CATHOLIC
BIBLE
STORIES
FOR CHILDREN

CATHOLIC BIBLE STORIES FOR CHILDREN

ANN BALL *with* **JULIANNE M. WILL**

Illustrated by **KEVIN DAVIDSON**

Our Sunday Visitor Publishing Division
Our Sunday Visitor, Inc.
Huntington, Indiana 46750

Nihil Obstat: Fr. Michael Heintz
Censor Librorum
Imprimatur: ✠ John M. D'Arcy
Bishop of Fort Wayne-South Bend
June 11, 2006

The *Nihil Obstat* and *Imprimatur* are official declarations that a
book or pamphlet is free of doctrinal or moral error. No implication is contained
therein that those who have granted the *Nihil Obstat* or *Imprimatur* agree with
the contents, opinions, or statements expressed.

The Scripture citations used in this work are taken from the *Catholic Edition of
the Revised Standard Version of the Bible* (RSV), copyright © 1965 and 1966
by the Division of Christian Education of the National Council of the Churches of
Christ in the United States of America. Used by permission. All rights reserved.

Our Sunday Visitor Publishing Division
Our Sunday Visitor, Inc.
200 Noll Plaza
Huntington, IN 46750

ISBN-13: 978-1-59276-243-9
ISBN-10: 1-59276-243-3 (Inventory No. T294)
LCCN: 2006924972

Cover and interior designs by Rebecca J. Heaston
Illustrations by Kevin Davidson

PRINTED IN CHINA

CATHOLIC
BIBLE
STORIES
FOR CHILDREN

Presented to:

Oona Ginty Pecson

By:

Nana

Date:

Christmas 2006

TABLE OF CONTENTS

INTRODUCTION

Dear Children,

You are about to begin a wonderful adventure with God.

The Bible is like a series of love letters from God, where you will read his stories of love for you and all people. You will discover that God speaks to you as a friend. Jesus praised children and wanted them to be near him. "Let the children come to me...for the kingdom of heaven belongs to such as these" (Mt 19:14).

In your Bible, you will meet God the Father. You will walk with Adam and Eve in the Garden of Eden and watch them eat the fruit that God had told them not to eat. You will see them sadly leave the beautiful garden because of their sin. But God still loved them and planned a way to save them.

You will travel with Noah in his ark during 40 days of rain. A dove comes back to him afterward, bearing an olive branch. The storm passes, and God's rainbow fills the sky.

Next, Abraham appears before you. He accepts God's love and believes in his promises that he will be the father of a great people. One of his great-great-grandsons, Joseph, will charm you with his red, white, blue, orange, and gold coat. His brothers sell him into slavery. He wins his freedom and becomes a leader in Egypt. In love, he forgives his brothers and gives them fine homes.

Then, you will meet the mighty Moses. God chose him to free his people from slavery in Egypt. You will feel the thrill of the great escape of God's people from Egypt. You will journey with them to Sinai, where God gives them the Ten Commandments. These are rules of love. Lots of excitement fills their camp when food falls from heaven to show God's care for them.

You will feel the passing of time and the people's joy in receiving the great King David to rule them. He is a close friend of God's. As a boy, he was a shepherd. As a king, he composed the Song of the Shepherd (Psalm 23).

The years fly by, and other pictures flash before you: the three young people in the fiery furnace and young Daniel in the lions' den. God is always present to them and rescues them.

Your adventure starts over with the coming of Jesus. You will hear the conversation between the Angel Gabriel and Mary. She will be Christ's mother. The Christmas scene at Bethlehem will welcome you. See yourself kneeling before Jesus with the shepherds and the wise men. Find yourself standing in the Temple, and hear old Simeon sing a lullaby to the baby Jesus. Twelve years later, return to that temple with Joseph and Mary, who worry that they have lost Jesus. All these stories show that Jesus is the savior promised to all your friends in the Old Testament.

The next time you see Jesus, he is an adult. His cousin John is baptizing him in the Jordan. Soon, you hear Jesus telling great stories about how much God loves people. He performs a bread miracle on a mountain and a wine miracle at a wedding. He heals ten lepers. You watch Jesus and the apostles at the Last Supper, when Jesus made the Holy Eucharist for you and all his friends.

Then, Jesus is treated badly and led to death on a cross. He had said the greatest love is to die for your friends, to save them from sin. On Easter, you can stand near his tomb. As the sun rises, you can see the stone rolled away and watch Jesus rise from the dead. Your adventure in the Bible continues with the birth of the Church at Pentecost. You will see the conversion of Paul and the glorious spread of the Church.

That story of love continues today in your family and in your parish church. Every year, you will hear these stories of love from your family and at your church. Lest you forget them, you have this precious Bible to read them again.

As you read your Bible, thank Jesus for his love. Tell him how much you love him, his Father, and the Holy Spirit. Tell his mother Mary how glad you are that she gave you Jesus. Ask her for a motherly hug.

And, above all, remember this: your adventure with Christ will last for the rest of your life. That's why we call it Good News!

— Fr. Alfred McBride, O.Praem.

Welcome

Hello, kids!

This book, a special version of the Holy Bible, was written especially for you, to help you learn about God's love for all mankind.

Meet Ichthus (Ik' thus). He is a Christian fish. The people who were followers of Jesus not long after he was crucified – the early Christians – were often attacked by the Romans. Those early Christians used a special picture of a fish as a password when they met someone new, to see whether he or she was a Christian, too. They used a fish because Jesus was called a fisher of men, capturing their hearts. The Greek letters inside spell "fish": each letter also stands for the words "Jesus Christ, Son of God, Savior."

You will find Ichthus on many pages in this book, along with stories and drawings to help you discover just how great God's love is. So follow Ichthus and dive right in!

Your friends,
Ann, Julianne, and Kevin
The Writers and the Artist

A special thank you to Max Ball, our junior editor on this project.

THE BIBLE: THE STORY OF GOD'S LOVE FOR US

God made us and loves us. He wants us to follow him and to live with him forever. God wants us to get to know him.

How do we know about God's love and his promises to us? A very special book called the Bible tells us about God and his plan. The Bible is a story of God's love for us. This holy book was written long ago, in the time before and after Jesus was here on earth.

> Let's go learn more about God's love for us.

The Bible is also called "Scripture," and it is really many books combined into one. Many different writers wrote these books, but each wrote with God's help. We call that help "inspiration." These books of the Bible are split up into two parts, or testaments. The word "testament" means "truth-telling." The books of the Old Testament describe how God created the world and all that happened in the world until Jesus was born. The books of the New Testament tell about Jesus' time on earth and his lessons on how to live in heaven with him.

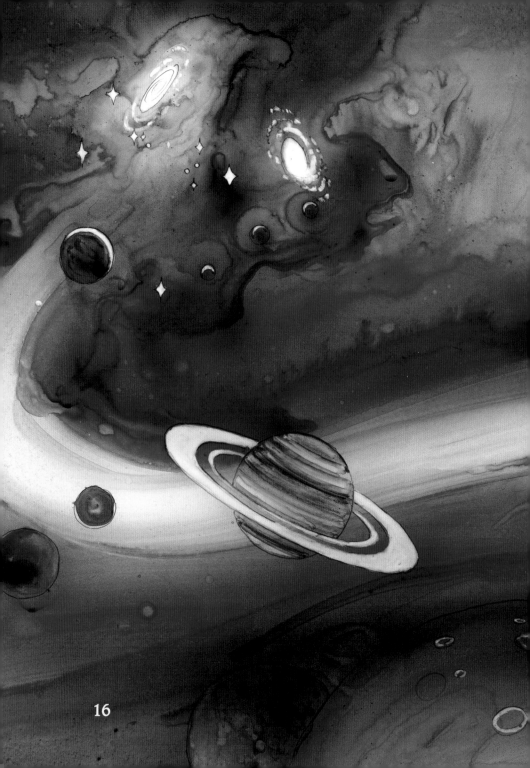

I.

IN THE TIME
BEFORE JESUS

GOD CREATES THE WORLD
(Genesis 1:1-31)

In the beginning, there was only God. Everything was dark before God created heaven and earth.

Then God said, "Let there be light," and there was light. He called the light "day," and he called the darkness "night." This was the first day.

18

Second, God made the beautiful
sky, and he separated it from
the world below.

Third, God created water
and land. He made many
plants and trees, too, and
they grew wonderful fruit.

Next, God made the sun, the
moon, and the stars, and put
them in the sky. God looked
at what He had done and
saw how great it was.

19

Then God made all
kinds of fish and birds
and animals to live on the
land and in the water. He made
them able to have baby fish and
birds and animals, so they could
fill the wonderful world he had made.

God looked at what he had made and saw
how beautiful it was. He wanted to share his
beautiful creation and his love with someone
like himself. So God made the first man and
woman to live on his earth and to share his
love. He called the first man Adam and the
first woman Eve. God told them to marry and
have children, and to enjoy the things he had
made.

At last, God was finished. He looked at what
he had done, and it was very good. So on the
seventh day, he rested.

God also blessed the seventh day. He made it
a holy day to rest from work, a day to relax
and enjoy all the good things he has given
us.

EDEN:
THE BEAUTIFUL GARDEN
(Genesis 2:4-23; 3)

God made a beautiful garden in Eden and gave it to Adam and Eve, our first parents. In the center of the garden was a tree with very special fruit. The person who ate that fruit would know what was good and evil. God allowed Adam and Eve to eat the fruit of any tree in the garden, except that tree with the special fruit.

But there was a sneaky serpent in the garden. He tempted Eve, telling her that the fruit from the tree of knowledge was the sweetest fruit in the garden. The serpent said if she ate it, she would be like

a god, because she would know
good and evil.

Eve ate the fruit and gave some of it to
Adam. Adam and Eve knew that they had
disobeyed God and tried to hide. But God
knows everything, and
Adam and Eve could
not hide from him.

When God saw that Adam and Eve had disobeyed him, he sent them out of the beautiful garden. He told them that they would have to work hard for food now. God punished the serpent, too, making the snake crawl on its belly.

Adam and Eve left the beautiful garden to go work in the world. They had children, and their children had children, and their children's children had children. Soon, many people lived on the earth. Everyone was banned from the Garden of Eden because of Adam and Eve's sin.

SIN AND GOD'S MERCY

When we do something wrong, our sin hurts God. But God loves us very much and is willing to forgive us when we are sorry. If we confess our sins, apologize to those we hurt and to God, and try to do better, God will show us his mercy. His Son, Jesus, died on the cross for our sins, and God wants us to be with him in heaven.

NOAH AND THE GIANT FLOOD
(Genesis 6-8)

The children and grandchildren of Adam and Eve had filled the earth. But many of them were very wicked, mean people, destroying God's beautiful work, and God grew very sad. Only one man, Noah, was good and obeyed God.

God told Noah that he had decided to flood the earth to wash away everything evil. He asked Noah to build a huge boat, called an "ark," that Noah and his family could live on until the floodwaters went down. God told Noah to bring birds and animals, too. "You shall bring two of every sort into the ark, to keep them alive with you," God said. "Also take with you every sort of food that is eaten, and store it up; and it shall serve as food for you and for them."

Noah made a huge ark for his family and filled it with animals and food. Soon, the rain began to fall. It rained, and rained, and rained — for 40 days and 40 nights, it rained. Finally, the rain stopped, but Noah and his family floated on the sea in the ark full of animals for many days after.

At last, God created a strong wind to begin drying the earth. Noah sent a dove out of the ark to see whether it could find dry land. The dove came back with a branch from an olive tree in its mouth. Now Noah, his family, and the animals could leave the ark.

Noah's children had children and grandchildren. Soon the earth was full of Noah's descendants, as well as many birds and animals. God made a promise to Noah, a "covenant": He would never flood the earth again.

God made a promise, a covenant, with Noah.

GOD TESTS ABRAHAM
(Genesis 12-22)

Abraham, a descendant of Noah, lived with his wife, Sarah, in a place called Haran. Abraham and Sarah wanted children very much, but they were sad because God had not sent them any.

One day, God told Abraham to leave Haran. He promised Abraham many blessings if he obeyed and said he would have as many descendants as there were stars in the sky. Abraham did not understand how Sarah, who was very old, could have a baby, but he trusted God and obeyed him. Abraham and Sarah left Haran and traveled to a place called Canaan. Abraham built an altar there for God. God blessed him, and Abraham became very rich.

Then, just as God had promised, Sarah had a baby. Abraham and Sarah were overjoyed. They loved their son, Isaac, very much.

28

When Isaac grew older, God decided to test Abraham to see just how much he loved God, and whether he would still obey. God told Abraham to take Isaac out to the desert and kill him as a sacrifice to God.

Abraham was terribly sad. How could he hurt the son he loved so very much? But Abraham loved God more and trusted him, so Abraham took Isaac out to the desert and prepared to kill his son, as God had asked. Just in time, God sent an angel to stop Abraham. He had passed the test! God saw that Abraham loved him enough even to give up his only son. Abraham loved Isaac very much, but he loved God first.

Abraham was filled with joy — he could keep his son! God promised Abraham and his family many blessings. Abraham and Isaac left the desert together and went home to Sarah. God kept his promise, called a "covenant," because Abraham obeyed God. He sent many blessings to Abraham and Isaac, and Isaac's children, and their children, and all the descendants of Abraham.

JOSEPH'S COAT
OF MANY COLORS
(Genesis 39-45)

Isaac's son Jacob had twelve boys. All
worked together as shepherds, tending their
family sheep. Jacob loved all his sons. But his
youngest boy, Joseph, was Jacob's favorite.
Jacob gave Joseph a beautiful coat of many
colors. The other sons grew very jealous of
Joseph and his beautiful new coat.

They also were angry with Joseph because of the dreams he had been having. In one dream Joseph saw the sun, the moon, and eleven stars bowing down to him. His brothers said it sounded like Joseph expected them to bow down to him. They grew even angrier.

God stays with his people wherever they are.

One day, the brothers were working in the field when Joseph came with a message from their father. The brothers saw Joseph coming in his beautiful coat and became so angry and jealous that they thought about killing him. Instead, they sold Joseph to some travelers who wanted to put Joseph to work in Egypt. Joseph's brothers tore the beautiful coat his father had given him. Joseph's father thought Joseph was dead, and he was very sad.

Joseph was a good worker, and almost everyone who knew him in Egypt liked him. But one day he met a mean woman who grew angry when he would not do the bad things she wanted him to do. So she made up a ter-

rible lie about him and had Joseph put in jail.
While Joseph was in jail, his friends there
talked to him about their dreams. Joseph had
a gift for dreams. He was able to tell his
friends what their dreams meant and what
would happen in the future. Everyone was
excited about Joseph's gift, and soon he was
famous.

One night, the ruler of the land of Egypt,
called the "pharaoh," had a dream that no
one could understand. So the pharaoh called

Joseph out of jail and asked him what his dream meant.

Joseph explained that soon there would be a famine. There would not be enough food for everyone unless they were very careful and saved extra food for the next few years.

The pharaoh was impressed with this wise young man. He put Joseph in charge of storing the food for Egypt. Joseph became one of the pharaoh's good friends.

Seven years later there was a great famine, just as Joseph had said. Egypt was the

only land that had food, thanks to Joseph, who had stored more than enough.

But in Canaan, Joseph's father and brothers quickly ran out of things to eat. Jacob sent his sons to Egypt to buy grain. They didn't know their brother Joseph was the one in charge of the grain, but he recognized his brothers at once. Joseph put them in jail.

The brothers talked among themselves in jail. They said being in jail was a punishment from God for the mean thing they had done to their brother Joseph many years ago. They said they were sorry for their sin. When Joseph heard this, he was very happy.

After Joseph was sure his brothers were truly sorry, he surprised them by telling them, "I am your brother, Joseph, whom you sold into Egypt. And now do not be distressed, or angry with yourselves, because you sold me here; for God sent me before you to preserve life." This shocked the brothers, because now Joseph was a very powerful friend of the pharaoh.

The brothers were very, very happy to see Joseph. They hurried home to tell their father, Jacob, that Joseph was alive. He was overjoyed, and the whole family moved to Egypt.

MOSES AND THE
GREAT ESCAPE
(Exodus 1-14)

After the death of the kind pharaoh who became Joseph's friend, an evil man took his place as leader of Egypt. This pharaoh was very jealous of Joseph's descendants, the Israelites. He made them slaves of the Egyptians and told his soldiers to kill all their baby boys.

One mother hid her baby boy from the soldiers. She put him in a basket at the edge of the river, where he would be safe. Soon, the pharaoh's daughter came to the river and found the baby boy. She decided to take him home and named him Moses, which means "pulled out of the water."

Moses grew up in the pharaoh's palace, strong, healthy, and good. Because he had a loving heart, Moses grew angry when he saw one of the pharaoh's soldiers hurting an Israelite slave. He told the soldier to stop hurting the man, but the soldier didn't listen. To save the slave, Moses killed the soldier. Moses knew the pharaoh would punish him for this, so he ran away to a different land and became a shepherd.

Moses was out in the field caring for his sheep one day when he saw a burning bush and went to investigate. To his surprise, even though the bush burned, the leaves stayed green! Then he realized that God was speaking to him.

God told Moses that the Israelites were suffering in Egypt as the slaves of the pharaoh. "I will send you to Pharaoh that you may bring forth my people, the sons of Israel, out of Egypt," God said.

Moses was afraid. "Who am I that I should go to Pharaoh, and bring the sons of Israel out of Egypt?" he said.

But God told Moses that he would help him perform many miracles to make the pharaoh listen. So Moses and his brother Aaron went to Egypt to free the Israelites.

When Moses went before the pharaoh and told him to let God's people go, Pharaoh said, "I do not know the Lord, and moreover I will not let Israel go."

Moses threw his walking stick on the ground, and it turned into a snake. The pharaoh was surprised, but he refused to set the slaves free.

The next day, Moses and Aaron met the pharaoh by the river and asked him again to let the people go. Again, Pharaoh refused. This time, Aaron threw his stick in the river, and the water turned to blood! This made the pharaoh angry because no one could drink the water, so he began to punish the Israelites even more.

Nine more times, Moses told the pharaoh to let his people go. Nine more times, Pharaoh refused. Nine times, bad things happened to the Egyptians. Frogs and locusts covered the land. The sky became dark, and the sun did not shine. Each time, the pharaoh would become frightened and promise to let the Israelites go. But each time, as soon as the problem was over, he changed his mind.

Finally, God told Moses that the Israelites should mark their doors with a special sign. That night, the Angel of Death came to Egypt. It took the oldest child of each Egyptian family, but passed by the Israelites' houses marked with the sign.

The Angel of Death even took the pharaoh's son. This was too much for the pharaoh, and he told Moses to take the Israelites out of Egypt. Quickly, the Israelites headed off toward the Red Sea before Pharaoh could change his mind again.

Soon, however, the pharaoh became angry. He wanted to punish the Israelites, and he sent his large army to bring them back.

How frightened the Israelites were! The sea was in front of them, and the army was behind them. Moses asked God what to do. Suddenly, a dark cloud came down, and the Egyptian army could not see the Israelites!

A strong wind blew the water aside.

God told Moses to hold his hand out over the Red Sea. A strong wind came and

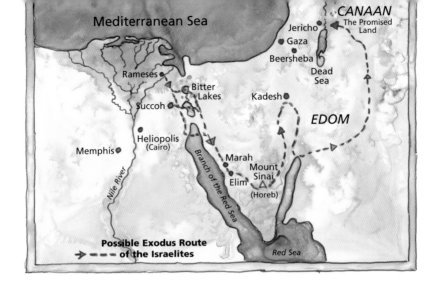

blew the water aside, making a dry path so the Israelites could cross over. Quickly, they ran across to safety. Then God told Moses to hold his hand over the sea again. Just as the Egyptian army got to the middle of the path across the sea, the waters rushed back, washing away the army.

The Israelites were saved. At last, God's people were free!

The night when the Angel of Death passed by the Israelites' homes is called "Passover." Even today, Hebrew people all over the world celebrate the night their children were saved.

BREAD FROM HEAVEN
(Exodus 16)

After Moses led the Israelites across the Red Sea, they found themselves in a large wilderness. The people began to worry, because there was no food. But the Lord spoke to Moses, and Moses reminded the people to trust God. He told them that God had promised to lead them to a new land, full of milk and honey and all good things.

The people said their prayers and, feeling sad, tired, and hungry, went to bed. What would happen to them?

What a surprise! The next morning, strange white flakes covered the ground. The people asked Moses what the white flakes were. "It is the bread which the Lord has given you to eat," replied Moses. The people gathered the strange new food, called "manna," and ate it.

Food came down from heaven for five days. On the sixth day, enough food fell for two days so the people would not have to work on the Sabbath, the Lord's day of rest. The people wandered in the wilderness for 40 years, and God sent food from heaven every day. God would not let his people go hungry!

THE TEN COMMANDMENTS
(Exodus 20)

While the Israelites were in the wilderness, God called Moses to the top of a mountain and gave him ten rules. These rules are the Ten Commandments, sometimes called the Decalogue. They tell God's people how to behave. We still follow these rules today.

God told Moses that those who obeyed his commandments would be blessed.
Many years later, the Israelites reached the land God promised, full of milk and honey and all good things.
Their trust in God was rewarded.

BAALAM'S DONKEY
(Numbers 22-24)

The Israelites settled in a place called Moab. This worried the king of Moab, because the Israelites were a very big group. The king, Balak, called for a man named Baalam and told him to come and curse the Israelites to make them move away. "I know that those you bless are indeed blessed, and those you curse are cursed," King Balak said to Baalam. So Baalam got on his faithful donkey and set off on a journey to curse the Israelites.

All of a sudden, the donkey walked off the road. Baalam was confused; he smacked the

donkey and made her get back on the road. But the donkey went off the road again, this time on the other side. Now Baalam was very angry, and he hit the poor donkey a second time. The donkey got back on the road, but instead of walking, she simply sat down. Baalam began to hit her again.

> Sometimes God uses animals to teach us a special lesson.

Just then, the donkey spoke. She said, "What have I done to you, that you have struck me these three times?"

Baalam was surprised to hear the donkey speak. Baalam said, "You have made sport of me. I wish I had a sword in my hand, for then I would kill you."

But the Lord opened Baalam's eyes, and he saw an angel standing in the road with a large sword, ready to stop Baalam before he would curse the Israelites. The angel told Baalam that his donkey had saved his life. "If she had not turned aside from me, surely just now I would have slain you and let her live."

Baalam felt very ashamed and thought about turning around to go home. But instead, the angel sent him to King Balak with a message.

When Baalam arrived, King Balak took him out to curse the Israelites. But God put words of blessing in Baalam's mouth instead of curses.

Three times the king told Baalam to curse the Israelites, and three times Baalam blessed God's chosen people instead. This made the king very angry! But Baalam would only say what God wanted him to say. He told the king that the people of Moab would be cursed instead. Then Baalam and his faithful donkey went home.

ISRAEL WANTS A KING
(1 Samuel 8-16)

The people of Israel wanted a king. They saw that other nations had kings and thought they should have one, too. They called their wisest man, Samuel, and asked him to find a king to lead their people.

Samuel told the people that a man named Saul would be their first king. Saul did become king, but sadly, he was not a very good king. God told Samuel that the next king would be one of the sons of a man named Jesse, who lived in Bethlehem.

So Samuel went to Bethlehem. He invited Jesse and his eight sons to come with him to make a sacrifice to the Lord. He took along special oil to anoint, or bless, a new king. When all eight of Jesse's sons gathered around Samuel, God told Samuel to anoint David, the youngest. So Samuel poured the oil on David's head, and the Holy Spirit came to David that day.

DAVID, THE KING WHO SANG
(1 Samuel 16:14-1 Samuel 31;
2 Samuel 1-2 Samuel 5:1-5)

King Saul was very sad. He had not been a good king for the Israelites, and he had disobeyed God. Saul asked his servants to find someone to cheer him up.

Saul's servant brought Jesse's son David, a young shepherd

boy who often sang to his sheep to keep them quiet. David sang and played music for Saul, which made him very happy.

At this time the Israelites were fighting another group called the Philistines. The Philistines had a very strong, very large soldier named Goliath. Goliath thought he could beat anyone, so he told the Israelites to send a man to fight him. But the Israelites were afraid of the giant.

David was delivering food to his brothers on the battlefield when he heard Goliath roar out his challenge. David did not like to see the Israelites so frightened by the giant, so he said he would fight him.

"No," said King Saul. "You are but a youth, and he has been a man of war."

But David was not afraid. "The Lord who delivered me from the paw of the lion, and from the paw of the bear, will deliver me from the hand of this Philistine."

Sadly, King Saul agreed to let the brave young boy fight. He gave him a sword and the clothes of a soldier. But David did not like the soldier's clothes and the sword. Instead he chose a slingshot and five smooth stones.

As the giant raced toward David with his mighty sword, David used his slingshot to shoot a stone at Goliath. The rock hit the giant smack in the middle of the forehead and knocked him down at once.

When the Philistines saw what happened, they ran and left the Israelites in peace. Young David was a hero.

David became king of the House of Judah. Later, when King Saul died, David became the king of all the Israelites in the city of Jerusalem. He was a holy ruler.

David never forgot the days when he was a shepherd boy and sang many beautiful songs honoring God. The words to some of David's songs are written in the Bible, where we can read them today. David's songs are called the Psalms.

One of David's songs compares God to a good shepherd who takes care of his sheep.

The 23rd Psalm

The LORD is my shepherd; I shall not want.
He makes me lie down in green pastures,
He leads me beside still waters,
He restores my soul.
He leads me in paths of righteousness
for his name's sake.
Even though I walk through the valley
of the shadow of death,
I fear no evil; for thou art with me;
thy rod and thy staff, they comfort me.
Thou preparest a table before me in the presence
of my enemies;
thou anointest my head with oil, my cup overflows.
Surely goodness and mercy shall follow me
all the days of my life,
And I shall dwell in the house of the LORD for ever.

Another one of David's songs reminds us that God wants us to be happy and serve him with joy.

Psalm 100

Make a joyful noise unto the LORD,
all the lands!
Serve the LORD with gladness!
Come into his presence with singing!

Know that the LORD is God!
It is he that has made us, and we are his;
we are his people, and the sheep of his pasture.

Enter his gates with thanksgiving,
and his courts with praise!
Give thanks to him, bless his name!

For the LORD is good;
his steadfast love endures for ever,
and his faithfulness to all generations.

A WISE KING
(1 Kings 1-11)

When King David died, his son Solomon became king. Soon after young Solomon took the throne, God appeared in a dream and told him to ask for whatever he wanted. Solomon asked God to make him wise, to know right from wrong, so he could be a good king. God was very pleased that Solomon did not ask for riches or other silly things, so he made Solomon the wisest man alive.

One day, two women came to Solomon, fighting over a baby. Each woman said the baby was hers. Wise Solomon listened to their arguments, then said, "Bring me my sword." When a servant brought his sword, Solomon said, "Divide the living child in two, and give half to the one, and half to the other."

The first woman was horrified. "Oh, my lord, give her the living child, and by no means slay it," she said. She would rather give up

the baby than see him killed. But the other woman didn't care. "It shall be neither mine nor yours; divide it," she said.

At this, Solomon said, "Give the living child to the first woman, and by no means slay it; she is its mother." Solomon knew that the real mother was the one who loved the baby so much she would rather give him up than see him killed.

Solomon loved God and ruled as a wise and good king for many years. He built a beautiful temple for God, and the people worshiped in peace. The whole world knew about Solomon's great wisdom and wealth.

Sadly, when Solomon was old, his wives turned his heart away from God. They led him to worship false gods. This made God very angry. He told Solomon that when he died, his great kingdom would be split. Only one tribe in the kingdom would be faithful. The Israelites would be punished, although not forever.

WORDS TO LIVE BY
(Proverbs)

King Solomon told his people many wise things. He wanted to teach them how to live well. He wanted them to love God and to be good and fair. Here is some of the wisdom Solomon shared with his people.

(Proverbs 1:7)
If you trust God, you will be wise; fools hate learning and wisdom.

(Proverbs 6:6-11)
Don't be lazy. Look at the wise little ant. It gathers its food in the summer so it will have enough to eat in the winter.

(Proverbs 11:2)
If you are full of pride, you will trip and fall. Instead, be good and humble.

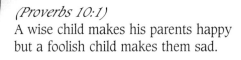

(Proverbs 10:1)
A wise child makes his parents happy but a foolish child makes them sad.

(Proverbs 14:16-17)
The wise person is cautious and turns away from evil. The fool doesn't pay attention and is careless.

(Proverbs 12:15-16)
A fool always thinks his own way of doing things is right. Instead, the wise person listens to advice.

(Proverbs 14:21, 31)
If you hate anyone, you are a sinner. But if you are kind to the poor, you will be happy. If you make things hard for the poor, you insult God. But if you are kind to the needy, you give God honor.

(Proverbs 15:1, 3)
A kind word turns away anger; a harsh word stirs up trouble. The eyes of God are always watching. He sees what is good and what is evil.

(Proverbs 15:13)
A happy heart keeps a smile on your face.

(Proverbs 16:4)
The Lord has made everything for a purpose.

65

(Proverbs 16:24)
Pleasant words are like
honey. They are sweet-
ness to the soul and
health to the body.

(Proverbs 17:9)
If you forgive others' mistakes,
you will make friends. If you
just think about disagreements,
you will make enemies.

(Proverbs 19:11)
If you have good sense, you will be slow to
get angry. It is better to ignore an offense.

(Proverbs 17:22)
A cheerful
heart is good
medicine.

(Proverbs 19:21)
You may think of
many plans, but
it is God's plan
that will be
carried out.

(Proverbs 20:11)
Even little children
are known by what
they do.

(Proverbs 22:1-2)
A good name is better than
many riches. God made the
rich and poor alike.

(Proverbs 28:1)
The wicked run away even when
there is no one after them. The
good are as bold as a lion.

(Proverbs 28:27)
Whoever gives to the
poor will lack nothing.

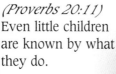

(Proverbs 30:5)
The word of God is true. He will
shelter those who take refuge in
him.

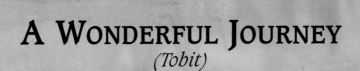

A WONDERFUL JOURNEY
(Tobit)

Tobit lived in Nineveh with his wife, Anna, and their son, Tobias. Although Nineveh was in a country where the people worshiped other gods, Tobit was faithful to God's law. He did many good things, giving food to the hungry and clothes to the poor. He always prayed and adored God.

An infection caused Tobit to go blind, so his wife, Anna, had to work to earn money. One day, however, Tobit remembered that a man who lived in a far-away town owed him some money, and he decided to send his son, Tobias, to get it.

God's angels guard us.

Anna cried, afraid her son would be harmed during the trip. Tobit reminded her that God always protects those who love and serve him. Still, because she was afraid, Tobit told Tobias to hire a man to go with him. Tobias found a man who agreed to go with him. He did not realize that the man was one of God's angels, Raphael.

Tobias and Raphael set off to get the money. When they came to the Tigris River, a large fish jumped up. Raphael told Tobit to catch it, so they could have some supper. He also told Tobias to save part of the fish to cook later as special protection against evil. He could use another part of it as a cure for his father's blindness.

When Tobias and Raphael stopped for the night at the home of some friends, Tobias met a beautiful woman named Sarah, who would become his wife. An evil spirit had followed her, but Tobias cooked part of the fish to send the spirit away, just as Raphael said he could.

After Tobias and Raphael got the money, they went back to their friends' house for Sarah, and the three traveled together to Tobias' home. When he arrived, Tobias used the other part of the fish to cure his father's blindness — just as Raphael said he could.

Tobit was so happy! He wanted to pay extra money to the young man who traveled with Tobias. At that moment, Raphael told them that he was really an angel. Tobias and his family praised God! They reminded everyone that God is never far away from those who love and serve him.

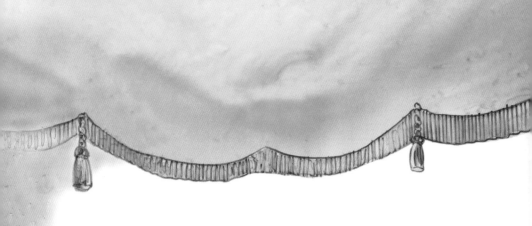

JUDITH SAVES HER PEOPLE
(Judith 8-16)

A bad general named Holofernes and his Assyrian army had surrounded the town of Bethulia, home of the Israelites. They would not let the people who lived there go in or out. Soon, the people of Bethulia ran out of food and water. They made their leaders promise to give in to the general and his army if God did not save them in five days.

One woman who lived in Bethulia, Judith, was wise and beautiful. She loved God and kept his commandments. Judith told the leaders their promise was foolish! She said they were wrong to give God a deadline to save

73

them. Then she prayed to God, and he gave her a plan.

Judith put on her nicest clothes and made herself very beautiful. Taking her maid with her, Judith left the town and went down to the army's camp. There, she pretended that she was going to help them figure out how to win the war against her people.

God helps his faithful people.

The general, Holofernes, saw how beautiful Judith was. On her fourth day in the camp, Holofernes held a great party in his tent. He drank too much wine and fell on his bed, asleep. All the servants left and went to their own beds, but Judith's maid stood by the door of the tent.

Judith prayed to God to give her strength to save her people. Then, she took Holofernes' sword and killed him. She and her maid slipped out of the tent and left the camp. The Assyrians thought the two women were just going out to pray, as they had done the past three days.

Instead, brave Judith and her maid returned quickly to their home in Bethulia. They told the townspeople what Judith had done. The people were surprised, and they prepared to go finish the battle. When the Assyrian army woke up and found what had happened, they were frightened and ran away. The people of Bethulia followed them and won the battle.

Judith began to sing a song of thanksgiving to God, and all the Israelites joined her in thanking and praising him. For as long as Judith lived, and for a long time after her death, the Israelites were at peace; no one tried to harm them.

ALEXANDER THE GREAT
(1 Maccabees 1-9)

Alexander was a great and mighty king. He ruled over much of the world. Instead of being a mean ruler, Alexander showed respect for all people. He allowed the Jews, God's chosen people, to keep God's laws and worship in the temple.

When Alexander was near death, he called his best officers and gave each of them a part of his kingdom. Each of his officers put on a crown and ruled over part of the kingdom. But some of the officers were bad rulers, and in many places, they began wars with God's people. They tried to force the Jews to break God's laws.

A BRAVE
AND GOOD FAMILY
(1 and 2 Maccabees)

One Jewish family, an old father named Mattathias and his five sons, remained faithful to God. They did many good deeds and became known as the Maccabees, which means "men who are as strong as hammers."

The Greek king had told the Jews that they must worship other gods, but Mattathias refused. He said he would not worship any but the one true God. Then Mattathias' son, Judas, and his other sons began to fight back against the king's orders. Judas got the rest of the Jewish people involved.

Many times, the small army of Jews had to fight larger armies. The enemy had many soldiers and even war elephants, trained to fight in battle. Judas told his men that they should not be afraid, because God was with them. His small army fought off the enemy, even with their elephants.

At last, the Jewish army won a big battle and got the temple of Jerusalem back. They were sad to find it dirty and falling apart. They started to work to clean it up and put it back in order. They lighted the holy lamp and celebrated for eight days.

JUDAS PRAYS FOR THE DEAD
(2 Maccabees 12:39-45)

After one battle between the king's soldiers and the Jews, Judas Maccabee sent his soldiers to gather up the bodies of the dead men and bury them properly. Judas and his men were sad to find that each of the dead men was wearing the symbol of a false god. This was a sin. Judas began to pray for the men so that their sin would be forgiven. He sent some money to the temple in Jerusalem as an offering. Judas knew there was a splendid reward for those who remain faithful to God, and he knew these sinners could still end up in heaven.

It is good to pray for those who have died.

If Judas did not expect these men to have the hope of heaven, it would be silly to pray for them. It was holy and pious to pray for these men.

THE FIERY FURNACE
(Daniel 3)

Three young Israelites were prisoners in Babylon when the ruler there, King Nebuchadnezzar, made a golden statue and told all the people that they must kneel down and worship it.

The three young men refused. They would
not worship any statue. They would only
worship the one true God.

The king called for the three Israelites and
demanded again that they kneel and worship
the statue. Again, they refused. This made
the king so angry that he ordered them to be
thrown into a blazing furnace.

The young men prayed to God as they stood
in the flames, trusting that he would protect

them. This made the king even angrier, so he made the fire hotter. All night, the king's workers added more fuel to the fire, which roared and crackled and gave off great heat.

The next morning, when the door to the furnace was opened, King Nebuchadnezzar peered inside. There, he saw four men, instead of three, walking around in the flames and singing praise to God.

The king commanded them to come out. The three Israelites walked out unharmed — not one hair on their heads was singed! God had protected them from the fire.

The fourth man in the fire disappeared. He was an angel, sent by God.

King Nebuchadnezzar was shocked. He began to praise God and honored those three young men, named Shadrach, Meshach, and Abednego.

God protects his faithful people.

DANIEL IN THE LIONS' DEN
(Daniel 6)

Daniel was a young Israelite who had been taken from his home to live in Babylon. Even though he was in a strange land, Daniel worshiped the one true God of the Jews and remained faithful.

Daniel was wise and could interpret dreams. Because of this, he became a very important man in the kingdom of King Darius. Some men grew jealous of Daniel's friendship with

the king, so they thought of a way to get rid of him. They tricked King Darius into making a rule that no one in the kingdom could pray to anyone but the king himself for 30 days. Anyone who broke that rule would be thrown into a cage of hungry lions.

Daniel knew about the rule, but he said his regular prayers to God anyway. Daniel would not stop worshiping God for anyone, even the king. When the king realized how he had been tricked, he was sad. But the law was the law, so Daniel was put into a cage with hungry lions, and a stone was placed in front of the door. The king said to Daniel, "May your God, whom you serve continually, deliver you!" Then the king went home, where he tossed and turned all night.

We honor and worship the one true God.

The next morning, King Darius raced to the lions' cage. He called out to

Daniel, and Daniel answered, "My God sent his angel and shut the lions' mouths, and they have not hurt me, because I was found blameless before him."

The king quickly let Daniel out of the lions'

cage, and the jealous men were put in his place. The lions quickly ate them up.

Then King Darius wrote to all the people in

his kingdom, telling them they should honor the God that Daniel worshiped. Kind Darius wrote, "for he is the living God, enduring forever, his kingdom shall never be destroyed." Daniel was saved because he trusted in God.

WHEN JESUS WAS ON EARTH

THE ANNUNCIATION: AN ANGEL BRINGS GOOD NEWS
(Luke 1:26-38)

After Adam and Eve disobeyed God in the Garden of Eden, every person was born in the shadow of their sin.

God's people waited and prayed for the day when He would send his Son to make up for this sin, so we could be in heaven with God. They believed that God's Son would come into the world as a mighty king. But God had other plans. He wanted to teach his people about his love.

In the little town of Nazareth, there lived a beautiful

The angel called Mary blessed among women.

girl named Mary. She was from a poor and simple family that loved God very much. Mary did not know it, but God had chosen her to be the mother of his Son. From the minute Mary began to grow in her mother's womb, her soul was clean and pure. She was the only person without the shadow of sin. This was the Immaculate Conception.

Mary became engaged to marry a man named Joseph. Joseph was a carpenter, a person who builds things from wood. He was a poor, simple, good man, who was happy to be marrying such a beautiful and holy girl.

One day before the wedding, an angel named Gabriel appeared to Mary. The angel greeted her and told her some wonderful news. God had chosen her to be the mother of his Son! Today, we remember the angel's words when we say the prayer known as the Hail Mary.

Mary was very surprised at the angel's news. But she loved God very much, so she said yes. She agreed to do whatever God asked. We call this her "fiat."

THE HAIL MARY

Hail Mary, full of grace!
The Lord is with you.
Blessed are you among
women,
and blessed is the fruit
of your womb, Jesus.
Holy Mary,
Mother of God,
pray for us sinners now,
and at the hour
of our death.
Amen.

St. Joseph's Big Job
(Matthew 1:18-25)

One night, an angel came to Joseph and told him a great secret. The angel said Mary was going to have a baby. She would be the mother of the new king, the savior of Israel, their people. This new king would redeem the people and wash away their sins.

Joseph was worried. He thought maybe Mary already had a husband.

But the angel knew at once what Joseph was thinking. "Joseph, son of David, do not fear to take Mary as your wife, for that which is conceived in her is of the Holy Spirit," the angel said. "She will bear a son, and you shall call his name Jesus, for he will save his people from their sins."

So Joseph and Mary were married. When they had to travel to Bethlehem, Joseph made

Mary comfortable on the long journey and
found a warm stable where Baby Jesus could
be born.

While they were there, an angel came to
warn Joseph of danger, so the new father

took Mary and the baby to Egypt, where they would be safe until they could return to their home in Nazareth.

Joseph cared for Baby Jesus, played with the little boy, and taught Jesus how to be a carpenter and make things out of wood. Joseph also taught Jesus the Jewish law and took him to the temple.

All his life, Joseph was a good husband and father to Mary and Jesus. We call him the foster father of our Lord. Now, St. Joseph is with his family again in heaven.

Joseph took care of the Holy Family on earth and he cares for us in heaven.

Just as Joseph took care of the Holy Family on earth, he helps take care of God's great family, the Church. Ask St. Joseph to help you grow up in God's love, just as he helped Jesus!

THE VISITATION:
MARY AND ELIZABETH
(Luke 1:5-25, 39-79)

Zechariah was a holy priest who served in the temple. He and his wife, Elizabeth, were good people who loved God very much. But they were sad because they did not have any children. They were old now and thought it was too late to have a baby.

One day while Zechariah was in the temple, the angel Gabriel came to him and told him that Elizabeth would have a son.

"How can this happen?" Zechariah said. "For I am an old man, and my wife is advanced in years."

"I am Gabriel, who stand in the presence of God," the angel answered. "You will be silent and unable to speak until the day that these

things come to pass, because you did not believe my words, which will be fulfilled in time."

Zechariah was very surprised at the angel's words. He was even more surprised when he left the temple and could not speak, just as the angel said.

Elizabeth soon learned that she was going to have a baby. She was very happy and thanked God for blessing her. She was to have a son, named John, just as the angel said.

We are blessed when we obey God.

Elizabeth and Mary were cousins. When Mary heard about Elizabeth's baby, she was full of joy for her cousin. Mary decided to visit, to share Elizabeth's happiness and see whether she needed help.

Mary walked to Zechariah and Elizabeth's home in the country. When she saw Elizabeth standing near her house, Mary ran to hug her. Just as Mary came near, the baby in Elizabeth's womb jumped. Elizabeth knew then that Mary was going to have a baby, too. Elizabeth knew that her own son, John, would honor Mary's baby, the Son of God. Elizabeth was filled with the Holy Spirit.

"Blessed are you among women, and blessed is the fruit of your womb!" Elizabeth said to Mary. "When the voice of your greeting came to my ears, the babe in my womb leaped for joy."

"My spirit rejoices in God my Savior," Mary said. "All generations will call me blessed; for he who is mighty has done great things for me, and holy is his name."

Mary stayed with her cousin Elizabeth, helping her for three months. At last, Elizabeth's baby, John, was born. Finally Zechariah was able to talk again! He went out and told everyone how wonderful and great God is.

THE BIRTH OF JESUS: A KING IS BORN

(Luke 2:1-20)

It was almost time for Joseph and Mary's baby to be born, and their little home was ready. Joseph had made a cradle for the baby to sleep in. Mary had made some little clothes for the baby and some blankets to wrap him in.

But Mary and Joseph were sad. They had to go on a very long trip soon, and they were worried that the baby might be born before they returned home.

Their home was a part of the Roman Empire, a land ruled by a man named Caesar Augustus.

Caesar wanted to take a census to count all the people he ruled. So everyone had to go to their hometowns to be counted. Joseph and Mary were descendants of King David, so they had to go to Bethlehem to be counted. Sadly, they began their trip.

When Joseph and Mary got to Bethlehem, the town was crowded. Everyone was there for the census. Joseph and Mary were tired from their long trip, but there was no place for them to stay. All the inns were full. Finally, a kind innkeeper told Joseph that he and Mary could sleep in the stable where the animals stayed. There was no bed, but there was clean hay to keep them warm.

So Joseph and Mary went to the stable and made a bed in the sweet-smelling hay. There was a little wooden manger to hold the food for the animals. Joseph put some clean hay in the manger to make a little bed for the baby who would soon arrive.

That night, Baby Jesus was born. Joseph and Mary wrapped him in soft blankets and put

him to sleep in the manger. How strange that
must have seemed. Here was a very special
baby, a new little king, sleeping in the hay.

There were some shepherds out in the field
that night with their sheep. An angel of God
came to them. At first, the shepherds were
frightened at the sight of this shining angel.
But then the angel spoke to them:

"Be not afraid; I bring you good news of a great joy which will come to all the people; for to you is born this day in the city of David a Savior, who is Christ the Lord."

105

More angels joined the first angel, and they all began to sing a beautiful song of praise to God.

The shepherds were amazed and happy at the news. They went to the town of Bethlehem and searched all the stables until they found a baby sleeping in a manger, just as the angel had said. They told Mary and Joseph about the angel's message. The shepherds knelt down and looked with love at the baby king. They thanked God for this blessing.

Mary remembered what the angel Gabriel had told her when he said she would have a baby. She kept the thoughts of these strange and wonderful happenings in her heart.

Hallelujah!

THREE KINGS:
THE GIFTS OF THE MAGI
(Matthew 2:1-22)

In the lands of the East, there were three very wise men. They were called Magi, or kings. These men knew about the earth and the stars. They also knew about God's promise to send a new king.

One day, the Magi saw a new star in the sky. They knew this meant that the new king was born. They wanted to honor him, so they set out on a long journey. The wise men followed the star, which led them to the land of Judah. When the Magi neared Bethlehem, they began to ask people where they could find the new king. Herod, the king of Judea, heard about

107

this and grew very nervous. He wanted to be the only king of the land. Herod called these visitors from the East to him.

"Go and search carefully for the child, and when you have found him come and tell me so I too may go and worship him," Herod said.

But Herod was lying. He didn't want to worship this new king. He wanted to get rid of Jesus. He hoped the Magi would help him find Jesus.

The Magi continued to follow the new star. At last, it came to rest over the place where Jesus was. The richly dressed kings from the East knelt down before him to show their love for the new little king.

The Magi brought the baby gifts of gold, frankincense, and myrrh. Frankincense makes a

beautiful smell when it is burned. Myrrh and gold were very expensive. These were gifts fit for a king.

That night the Magi all had a strange dream. An angel told them not to go back to King Herod, because he had lied and wanted to hurt Jesus. The Magi went home a different way without telling Herod where to find the baby.

Then Joseph had a dream. In his dream, an angel came to warn him about Herod and told him to leave Bethlehem. Joseph left with Mary and Baby Jesus that night. They escaped to Egypt, where they lived for several years.

When King Herod found out that the Magi had tricked him, he was very angry. Herod was jealous of the new little king. He told his soldiers to go kill all the children in Bethlehem younger than two years old, hoping that they would kill Baby Jesus, too. He didn't know the Holy Family had already escaped.

How the mothers and fathers of Bethlehem cried! Today we set aside a day, December 28, to remember these little children, called the Holy Innocents.

Finally, King Herod died. An angel came in a dream and told Joseph it was safe to go home. Joseph, Mary, and Baby Jesus could return to Nazareth at last.

The Bible does not list the names of these three kind men, but Sacred Tradition tells us that the names of the Magi were Caspar, Melchoir, and Balthazar.

THE PRESENTATION
IN THE TEMPLE
(Luke 2:21-40)

Mary and Joseph were Jewish and faithfully followed the laws of the Jewish religion. One of these laws said that baby boys should be taken to the temple in Jerusalem to be presented there. Their parents had to bring a gift, or sacrifice, usually two birds. When the time came, Mary and Joseph took Baby Jesus to the temple.

There was an old man in Jerusalem named Simeon who loved God and prayed all his life. Because Simeon was so faithful, God had promised Simeon that he would not die until the Redeemer came to earth. The Holy Spirit led Simeon to the temple on the very same day that Mary and Joseph came to present Jesus.

When Simeon saw Jesus, his heart was full of joy. He knew that this baby was the Promised One sent by God. Simeon praised God and said, "Behold, this child is set for the fall and rising of many in Israel."

Then Simeon did a strange thing. He turned to Mary and said, "A sword will pierce through your heart." Simeon was warning Mary that something would happen to make her very sad. He wanted her to be prepared for Jesus' death on the cross.

An old woman named Anna was also in the temple that day. She was a prophetess, a person who could tell people what was going to happen in the future. When she saw Baby Jesus, she gave thanks to God. She told everyone in the temple that this baby was going to be the Redeemer for God's people.

Mary and Joseph were amazed at the things they heard. They thought about what Simeon and Anna said and kept the words in their hearts.

Today, the church sets aside a special day, February 2, to remember when Joseph and Mary took Baby Jesus to the temple. The feast is called the Presentation.

In some countries, people put new clothes on a little statue of Baby Jesus. They take the statue to their church and ask the priest to bless it. Then they take their statue home to remind them of the child Jesus.

Jesus' Home
at Nazareth

What was Jesus' home like? The Bible does not tell us much about the time when he was growing up. But scientists have learned much about the daily lives of the people who lived when Jesus did. We can imagine what it was like in his home from what scientists tell us about other homes.

Joseph worked hard to take care of Mary and Jesus. He played with Jesus when he was a child, and later taught Jesus how to be a carpenter, making furniture and other things out of wood. The Bible tells us that Jesus was good and obeyed his parents.

Jesus' house probably only had one room, with a cave at the back to store things in. It

was made of stone, with a flat roof covered
with stones and dirt. The floor likely was
made of stone, too. Nazareth had many hills
and was near the mountains.

In the morning, the family would get up and
roll up their bedding. Joseph, Mary, and Jesus
would start their day with a prayer, facing the
temple of Jerusalem. The family was Jewish,
so Joseph and Jesus would wear a special
prayer shawl over their shoulders and two
small boxes on their wrists and foreheads.
The boxes were made of parchment, a kind of
paper, and had the words to the prayer inside.
At night, the family would say the same

prayer to remind them that God would be with them as long as his people obeyed.

Next, the family would eat bread, fruit, and olives for breakfast, saying a blessing over their food. As Joseph and Jesus left for work, they would touch a little box on the door called a "mezuzah." This box also had a prayer inside. Then they would kiss their hands as a sign of respect for God and his promises.

Mary would wash the dishes and sweep the floor. Then, she would put a shawl on her head and take a jug down to the fountain in the center of town to get water for the family. Sometimes she would wash the family's clothes in the same fountain.

Next, Mary would grind wheat between two flat stones to make bread and take it to a big

116

oven in town. The family only had a small grill at home. Mary also took wool and flax and spun them into thread or yarn. Then she would take them to a man who would weave them into cloth.

At lunch, the family ate a big meal — bread, fruit, and meat or fish. They had wine to drink. In the evening, they had bread and vegetables or cheese.

After supper, Mary and Joseph would talk about God and teach Jesus the Law of Moses, the Psalms, and other stories of the Israelites. When it got dark, they would light a lamp, made with a piece of cloth or string in a dish of olive oil. After evening prayers, the family would unroll their bedding and go to sleep.

On Fridays, when the sun went down, Joseph and Jesus would go to the synagogue, a

building where Jewish people pray. Each home would have a candle in the window and a special candleholder, called a "menorah," on the table.

Saturday was called the "Sabbath." On Saturday mornings, the family would go to the synagogue for a special service. At noon, they returned home to eat the meal Mary had made the day before. The Jews did not work, even to make dinner, on the Sabbath. In the afternoon, they would take a little walk before going back to the synagogue for the vesper service. The Sabbath ended when the sun went down. Then the children would play in the streets while the men visited and talked, and the women went to the fountain for water.

A Holy Family, a happy family.

The Holy Family lived a simple, happy life in their little home in Nazareth.

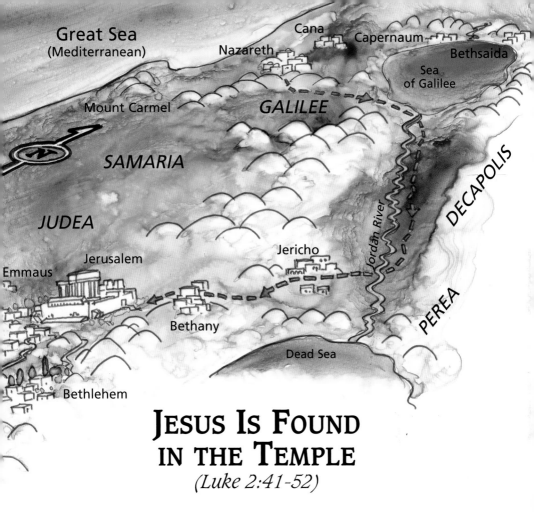

Great Sea
(Mediterranean)

Cana

Capernaum

Nazareth

Bethsaida

Sea
of Galilee

Mount Carmel

GALILEE

SAMARIA

DECAPOLIS

JUDEA

Jordan River

Jerusalem

Jericho

Emmaus

PEREA

Bethany

Dead Sea

Bethlehem

JESUS IS FOUND
IN THE TEMPLE
(Luke 2:41-52)

In his little home in Nazareth, Jesus grew tall
and strong in spirit. God's grace was with
him.

Each year, Mary and Joseph went on a long
trip called a "pilgrimage" to the temple in
Jerusalem with the other Jews. When Jesus

120

was twelve
years old, he
went with
Joseph and
Mary for the
first time to cele-
brate the Passover
there. At twelve, Jesus
was nearly old enough
to be a "Son of the
Law," or a grown man.

A group of men,
women, and children all
traveled together to

Jerusalem. Many were friends and relatives of
Joseph and Mary. They talked and visited
along the way, while the children played.

At last, they reached the holy city. There were special services in the temple, and incense was burned to make a sweet smell while everyone worshiped God. Later, the Holy Family ate a special Passover meal of roasted lamb, bitter herbs, and unleavened bread to remind them of the Israelites' escape over the Red Sea from Egypt.

After three days, the ceremonies were over. The little group of pilgrims gathered their tents and began the trip back to Nazareth. Joseph did not see Jesus, but he thought the boy was with his mother. Mary did not see Jesus. She thought Jesus was with Joseph and the other men.

But where was Jesus? In the temple! He wandered around, watching what was going on. Jesus was so interested that he lost all track of time. He began to listen to a group of men who were teaching. At first he stood quietly, then he sat down and began to ask them questions.

That night, Joseph began to look for Jesus.

Jesus was not with the men, so Joseph crossed to the women's camp to ask Mary if Jesus was with her, but he was not. Jesus was missing!

Joseph and Mary searched the entire camp, but they did not find Jesus. It was dark, so they lay down, praying to God that Jesus was safe. As soon as it was light, they got up and hurried back to Jerusalem.

They went everywhere asking about Jesus. Mary and Joseph prayed to God for help in finding him. They were frantic and frightened.

Jesus obeyed his parents.

Finally, after three days, Joseph and Mary came to the temple. There was Jesus! He was talking to the wise teachers.

Mary rushed up and hugged him. Then she said, "Son, why have you treated us so? Behold, your father and I have been looking for you anxiously."

Surprised, Jesus looked at his mother and said, "Did you not know that I must be in my Father's house?"

Joseph and Mary did not understand what Jesus meant. They did not realize that Jesus was talking about God, his Father in heaven.

Jesus went home with Joseph and Mary and obeyed them. Joseph and Mary were happy that Jesus was safe. They were glad that they had found little lost Jesus.

126

JOHN BAPTIZES JESUS
(Matthew 3, Luke 3:1-22)

John, the cousin of Jesus, lived in the countryside near the River Jordan. He began to tell people about God. He told them that they should be sorry for their sins, because God was soon going to send the Savior to make up for those sins. Those who were sorry went with John to the river, where he baptized them in the water. He was soon known as John the Baptist.

The people asked John whether he was the one God promised them, the one who would redeem God's people.

"I baptize you with water; but he who is mightier than I is coming," said John. "He will baptize you with the Holy Spirit and with fire."

The Holy Spirit came to Jesus.

They knew John was a great prophet, which means he could tell them about things that were going to happen. They wanted to

be ready for the kingdom of heaven.
When Jesus was 30 years old, He went to the
River Jordan to see his cousin, John. Jesus
asked John to baptize him, but John knew
that Jesus was the Son of God, the one he
had been preaching about. John was surprised
and said, "I need to be baptized by you, but
instead you come to me?"

But Jesus said, "Let it be so."

Then they walked into the river, and John
baptized Jesus with water. Then, the heavens
opened and the Holy Spirit, like a dove, came
down and landed on Jesus! A loud voice came
from heaven and said, "This is my beloved
Son, with whom I am well pleased."

The people were amazed. They knew then
that Jesus was the promised Redeemer, the
one who would die to make up for their sins.
Some of the people began to follow him and
to listen to what he was teaching. Jesus told
them to be sorry for their sins and to be more
loving, because it was time for the kingdom
of heaven to come to earth.

Jesus made his friends fishers of men.

JESUS CALLS THE APOSTLES
(Matthew 4:18-22, 10:1-15)

Jesus went to the Sea of Galilee to preach. There he saw two fishermen, brothers named Peter and Andrew. Jesus called to

them, saying, "Follow me, and I will make you fishers of men." Peter and Andrew left their fishing right away and followed Jesus to help teach about God's love.

Next, Jesus saw two other brothers, James

and John, in a boat with their father fixing their fishing nets. Again, Jesus called out and invited them to become fishers of men. He wanted them to help capture people's hearts with love for God. James and John also went with Jesus.

Many people began to follow Jesus around Galilee to hear him teach about God. Jesus knew he would need good friends to help spread his message, so he chose twelve men to go with him to learn about God and share his Good News. Peter, Andrew, James, and John were part of this group. Jesus also called Philip, Bartholomew, Matthew, Thomas, another man named James, Simon, Thaddeus, and Judas Iscariot. Jesus called these men his apostles.

Jesus sent the twelve apostles out to cure the sick and talk about the kingdom of God. He told them to take nothing with them on their trips. They had to trust God to give them what they needed on their journeys.

THE WEDDING AT CANA
(John 2:1-12)

Jesus and his family and friends were invited to a wedding at Cana, a town near his home in Galilee. There was a big meal, a feast for all the guests. During the celebration, Mary, Jesus' mother, heard that the bride and groom had run out of wine to drink. How embarrassing this would be! Mary told Jesus, "They have no wine." She wanted Jesus to help them.

Jesus tried to say no. He said it was not time yet to begin performing miracles.

But Mary knew that Jesus would help if she asked. She turned to the servants and said, "Do whatever he tells you."

Jesus told the servants to bring him some jars of water. Quickly, the servants filled six large stone jugs to the brim with water. Then Jesus told the man in charge of the feast to taste it. A miracle had happened! Jesus had turned the water into wine, even better than the wine they had served at the beginning of the wedding.

Jesus did as his mother asked him to do.

The wedding celebration was saved. When Jesus' apostles saw this miracle, they believed even more in his power.

JESUS TEACHES AND HEALS
(Matthew 5-7)

Everywhere Jesus went, people came to hear him. Many of those people were sick and asked Jesus to make them well. Jesus healed many of them. He explained that their belief in God had made them better. Jesus told them to be happy and rejoice because of God's goodness.

One day, Jesus went up on a mountain to teach the people who came to hear him. Here on the mountain, Jesus preached a special sermon. He told the people to be kind and good to everyone, even their enemies. Jesus told them to make peace with people who hurt them. He said those who love God are the light of the world, and that they must let that light shine. He told them God is love, and that they should rely on God to take care of them.

Then Jesus told the people about eight special blessings. We call these the Beatitudes. These blessings of Jesus are like promises for us.

The Beatitudes

"Blessed are the poor in spirit,
for theirs is the kingdom of heaven."

"Blessed are those who mourn,
for they shall be comforted."

"Blessed are the meek,
for they shall inherit the earth."

"Blessed are those who hunger and thirst
for righteousness, for they shall be satisfied."

"Blessed are the merciful,
for they shall obtain mercy."

"Blessed are the pure in heart,
for they shall see God."

"Blessed are the peacemakers,
for they shall be called sons of God."

"Blessed are those who are persecuted
for righteousness' sake, for theirs is the
kingdom of heaven. "

"Blessed are you when men revile you
and persecute you and utter all kinds of evil
against you falsely on my account. Rejoice and
be glad, for your reward is great in heaven."

THE LORD'S PRAYER
(Matthew 6:9-15, Luke 11:1-4)

One of his followers asked Jesus the best way to pray. This is the special prayer Jesus taught him and us:

Our Father, who art in heaven,
Hallowed be thy name.
Thy kingdom come,
Thy will be done
  On earth as it is in heaven.
Give us this day our daily bread,
And forgive us our trespasses,
  As we forgive those who trespass
  against us.
And lead us not into temptation,
  But deliver us from evil.
Amen.

A SPECIAL VISIT

(Luke 10:38-42)

One day, Jesus went to visit two sisters named Mary and Martha. When Jesus arrived, Mary sat down at his feet and listened to what he was saying. But Martha was distracted by many chores. She was cooking and cleaning to make certain everything was ready for the Lord's visit. After a while, she went to Jesus and said, "Lord, do you not care that my sister has left me to serve alone? Tell her to help me."

Jesus wanted Martha to understand how important it was to listen to God's word first, above everything else.

Jesus told her, "Martha, don't be worried and distracted by so many things. Mary has chosen the best thing, to hear what I am saying. What she learns cannot be taken away from her."

LOAVES AND FISHES
(Matthew 14:15-21, John 6:1-14)

Crowds of people had been listening to
Jesus teach all day near the Sea of Galilee.
It was almost time for dinner, and everyone
was growing very hungry. Jesus pointed this
out to his friends, the apostles.

"How are we to buy bread, so that these people may eat?" Jesus asked Philip. Philip replied that they didn't have the money to buy enough for everyone to have even a little. But Jesus had a plan.

Andrew told Jesus there was a boy in the crowd who had five barley loaves and two fish. "But what are they among so many?" Andrew asked. He didn't think that little bit would make any difference.

Jesus smiled and told his apostles to ask everyone to have a seat. Then Jesus took the two fish and the five loaves of bread and looked up to heaven. He blessed the food and told the apostles to begin feeding the people.

Because they believed in him, the apostles did as Jesus asked. They were surprised to see there was enough that everyone in the crowd could eat as much as they wanted. There was even enough left over to fill twelve baskets. It was a miracle!

When the people saw this, they said, "This is indeed the prophet who is to come into the world."

JESUS LOVES CHILDREN
(Luke 18:15-18)

Everywhere Jesus went, he attracted large crowds of people who wanted to hear him teach, ask him to cure their illnesses, or receive a blessing.

One day when Jesus was speaking, a group of mothers brought their children to him to be blessed. But the apostles told them to leave.

Jesus loves the little children,
All the children of the world.
Red and yellow, black and white,
All are precious in His sight.
Jesus loves the little children of the world.
— Words by the Rev. C.H. Woolston

Jesus was too busy with the adults, they said, and didn't have time for children.

When Jesus heard this, he was very unhappy with his friends. "Let the children come to me," he said, "for to such belongs the kingdom of God."

Jesus hugged and held the children. He put his hands on their heads and blessed them. The children knew Jesus loved them very much.

Jesus told the crowd: "Truly, I say to you, whoever does not receive the kingdom of God like a child shall not enter it." Jesus reminded the adults that they were all children of God, and that they must obey and love their Heavenly Father.

THE STORIES OF JESUS

Jesus was a wonderful teacher. Instead of telling people what to do, he told them stories. These stories made his lessons easy to understand and remember. We call Jesus' stories "parables."

Each parable has a message about how God wants us to live. Here are a few of Jesus' stories.

THE PARABLE OF A LAMP

(Matthew 5:15-16, Luke 8:16)

No one lights a lamp, then hides it under the bed. Instead, they put it on a table so that everyone who comes in the room can see the light.

In the same way, let your light shine before others. Do good works and give glory to God in heaven. Use the talents God gave you. Big or little, let your light shine.

150

THE PARABLE OF
THE SEEDS
(Luke 8:4-18)

A farmer went out to plant some seed. As he was throwing the seeds on the

ground, some fell onto the path and were eaten by birds. Some of the seeds fell on rocks and dried up in the sun. Some of the seeds fell into a patch of weeds and died in the shade. But some of the seeds fell on good ground. Those seeds grew tall and strong and had plenty of fruit.

Open your heart to Jesus.

Jesus said his words are like the seeds. Is our heart like the bad ground, where the seeds of Jesus' message will die? Or is our heart like the good soil, where his words of love can grow?

THE PARABLE OF THE MUSTARD SEED
(Luke 13:18-19)

J esus' listeners asked him to explain what
the kingdom of heaven is like. Jesus said it
is like a mustard seed — it starts out very,
very small, but if it is planted in good ground,
it will grow big enough for birds to make their
nests in.

THE UNFORGIVING SERVANT

(Matthew 18:21-35)

One day, a king sat counting how much his servants owed him. The king called in one servant who owed him a huge amount and told the servant he and all of his things would be sold to pay off the money.

The servant cried and fell on his knees in front of the king. "Have patience with me, and I will pay you everything," he said to the king.

The king felt sorry for the servant. He told him he would not have to pay his debt.

A few days later, that same servant went to one of his co-workers who owed him some money. "Pay what you owe," he said angrily.

The fellow servant fell down on his knees and said, "Have patience with me, and I will pay you."

But the man would not listen. He had his fellow servant thrown in jail.

The king was furious. "You wicked servant!" he said. "Should not you have had mercy on your fellow servant, as I had mercy on you?" He punished the servant.

Jesus said God is like the patient king; He will forgive us. But we must forgive others, too.

THE GOOD SHEPHERD
(Luke 15:1-7)

The people in charge of the government couldn't understand why Jesus spent time with sinners and people who collect taxes. They asked him why he would waste his time with those bad people. Jesus answered them with a parable.

A shepherd will leave his ninety-nine sheep alone in the desert to go looking for one lost sheep, Jesus said. "And when he has found it, he lays it on his shoulders, rejoicing. And when he comes home, he calls together his friends and his neighbors, saying to them, 'Rejoice with me, for I have found my sheep.'"

It is the same when one of God's people is lost because of sin, Jesus said. Like a good shepherd, Jesus watches those who are safe in God's love but he goes out to bring back a lost sinner. When a sinner is saved, there is great joy in heaven.

157

THE GREATEST COMMANDMENT
(Matthew 22:34-40)

The people knew that God had given Moses the Ten Commandments for them to live by. They asked Jesus which was the greatest commandment of all.

He said to him, "You shall love the Lord your God with all your heart,

and with all your soul, and with all your
mind. This is the great and first commandment. And a second is like it: You shall love
your neighbor as yourself. On these two commandments depend all the law and the
prophets."

THE TEN LEPERS
(Luke 17:11-19)

One day, ten men with a terrible disease called leprosy ran up to Jesus as he entered a village. "Jesus, Master, have mercy on us," they cried. Jesus had mercy on them and told them to go and show themselves to the priest. As they ran to the priest, they discovered a miracle — they were healed! Their disease was gone.

One of the men, a foreigner from another country, ran back to thank Jesus. He threw himself at Jesus' feet and praised God who made him well. Jesus was sad that only one of the men remembered to say "thank you." But he told the

thankful man to get up and go on his way.
Jesus said, "Your faith has made you well."

We should always have faith in God and
remember to tell him "thank you" for all the
good things he does for us.

THE LAST SUPPER:
JESUS SAYS GOODBYE
(Matthew 26:14-30, Mark 14:12-26,
Luke 22:1-39, John 13-17)

Jesus knew God was going to call him soon to die on the cross. Jesus gathered his friends together for one last supper. He wanted to prepare the apostles for the frightening days ahead.

The friends enjoyed a good meal. While they were eating, Jesus took some bread and blessed it. He broke it

into pieces and gave
it to his disciples. He
told them, "Take, eat; this
is my body."

Then Jesus took the cup of wine, gave thanks
to God, and blessed it. He said, "This is my
blood of the covenant, which is poured out
for many for the forgiveness of sins."

Jesus told his apostles that after he went
home to heaven, they should turn bread and
wine into his Body and Blood and give it to
his people. "Do this in remembrance of me,"
he said.

After supper, Jesus knelt down and washed

the apostles' feet. He wanted to show his love and to remind them how important it is to take care of one another.

Jesus knew there was one apostle at dinner that night who did not really love him. Jesus knew Judas Iscariot would tell the soldiers where to find him when they wanted to kill him. Jesus told Judas to go and do what he needed to do. The other apostles did not understand where Judas was going. But Jesus knew that Judas' betrayal was part of God's plan.

Jesus told his friends that he would be leaving them soon. He talked to them about how to keep spreading God's message after he was gone. But Jesus promised his friends he would come back and see them again. Then he and his apostles went out into a little garden to pray.

While the others were praying, Judas hurried off to make a deal. The soldiers and the government were going to pay Judas money so he would tell them where Jesus was.

Jesus' Great Promise
(John 6:47)

Jesus made a great promise to his people. He said, "Truly, truly, I say to you, he who believes has eternal life."

165

If we live as good Christians here on earth and believe in God's Word, we will go to heaven to live with God forever. Jesus gave us this great gift — everlasting life — by dying on the cross for our sins. His death made up for those sins that were keeping us from entering heaven.

If we live a good life on this earth, we can live again forever in happiness with God. Hallelujah!

Jesus made a promise.

JESUS DIES ON THE CROSS
(Matthew 27, Mark 15,
Luke 22-23, John 18-19)

Jesus prayed in a garden after his last supper with his friends, the apostles. He told God that he hoped he might not have to die on the cross, but that he would do whatever God wanted.

Soon, the Roman soldiers came to the garden and took Jesus prisoner. They took him to the chief priest, who asked Jesus if he thought he was the Son of God. Jesus said, "You say that I am." Others who had heard

Jesus preaching said that Jesus called God his Father. This was against the law. The chief priest said Jesus was guilty and would have to die. The people spit on him and hit him. They took him to the Roman governor, Pontius Pilate.

Pilate asked Jesus, "Are you the king of the Jews?" But Jesus only said, "You have said so."

Pilate said Jesus was not guilty. He asked the people whether he should let Jesus go, or let Barabbas, a murderer, out of jail. The people shouted that he should let Barabbas go and hang Jesus on the cross instead. Pilate said that Jesus was innocent, but the crowds kept shouting, "Crucify him!"

Pilate handed Jesus over to the soldiers, who beat him and made fun of him for preaching about the kingdom of heaven. They put a crown of thorns on his head. They put a sign on the cross that said, "Jesus of Nazareth, the King of the Jews."

The soldiers made Jesus carry his cross to the hill called Golgotha, where he would be crucified. The wooden cross was huge and very heavy, and Jesus fell three times while he carried it. The soldiers grabbed a nearby traveler named Simon and made him help Jesus. Veronica, a kind woman by the side of the road, wiped Jesus' face with her handkerchief.

At Golgotha, the soldiers made Jesus lie down on the cross and nailed him to it. Then they raised the cross and waited for Jesus to die.

Jesus' mother, Mary, and one of his friends,

John, were standing nearby. Jesus asked John to care for his mother, who was brokenhearted.

Jesus looked up to heaven and said, "Father, forgive them, for they know not what they do."

The soldiers also crucified two thieves, one on each side of Jesus. One of them was angry. Looking at Jesus, he said, "Are you not the Christ? Save yourself and us!" But the other thief said, "This man has done nothing wrong.... Jesus, remember me when you come into your kingdom." Jesus told the second man, "Today you will be with me in Paradise."

Finally, Jesus breathed his last breath and said, "It is finished." At that moment, there was a loud clap of thunder, and the curtain in the temple tore apart. The crowd was afraid and worried about what they had done.

Later that day, some friends of Jesus took his body off the cross, carefully wrapped it, and

laid it in a tomb, a cave carved out of
rock. A huge stone was rolled in front of
the opening. After staying there a while,
Jesus' sad friends went home.

Jesus Is Alive!
(Luke 24)

How sad Jesus' friends were after his death!

Two days later, on Sunday morning, some of the women went to Jesus' tomb. When they got there, they discovered that the huge stone blocking the entrance to the tomb had been rolled away. They looked inside, but the body of Jesus was gone. Instead, the women saw two angels in the tomb!

The women were frightened and bowed down. But the angels told them not to be afraid. They asked the women, "Why do you seek the living among the dead?"

174

Jesus was risen, they told the women.

The women ran back to tell the apostles the good news. Not all of Jesus' friends believed them. But Peter went to the tomb and was amazed to see that Jesus' body was gone.

That same day, two of Jesus' friends were walking to a town called Emmaus. Suddenly, a man joined them on their walk. It was Jesus! But they did not recognize him. Jesus talked to them about the Scriptures during their journey, and when they got to Emmaus, the two apostles asked Jesus to stay with them. During supper, Jesus took some bread and wine and blessed it. Finally, the two apostles recognized Jesus!

We can live forever!

With that, Jesus disappeared. The two friends ran back to Jerusalem where the other disciples were gathered and told them the good news. While they were talking,

Jesus appeared again. The other disciples were frightened and thought he was a ghost.

"Why are you troubled?" said Jesus. Then he showed them the marks of the nails in his hands and feet. They were overjoyed to see it was really Jesus, alive.

Jesus explained that everything happened just the way God planned it.

For 40 days after he rose from the dead, Jesus stayed on earth with his friends. One day, after blessing his apostles, he was lifted to heaven. The apostles were amazed and happy. They went back to Jerusalem praising God.

PENTECOST:
THE HOLY SPIRIT COMES
(Acts 1-2)

When Jesus came to see the apostles after he rose from the dead, he promised that God would send the Holy Spirit to his friends with a special gift. He told the apostles and Mary to go to Jerusalem to wait for the coming of the Spirit. Jesus then ascend-

ed into heaven, rising on a cloud to be with his Father.

The apostles and Mary went to Jerusalem, praying to God and praising him. They were gathered together when they heard a strong wind. The sound rushed in the windows and filled the house. Then a light that looked like a flame appeared over the heads of Mary and each of Jesus' friends. They were filled with the Holy Spirit and started to speak in different languages.

Many people in town heard the loud wind. They came running to see what was happening. The people in this town were from many different faraway places, but each heard Jesus' friends speaking in his own different language. They were amazed. The apostles were talking about the wonderful power of God.

"What does this mean?" shouted a man in the crowd.

Peter told the crowd that even though Jesus had died on the cross, he had come back to life. He told the people that God wanted everyone to be sorry for their sins and to be baptized in the name of Jesus. He told the people that they could be filled with the Holy Spirit, too. That very day, about 3,000 people were baptized.

The Holy Spirit comes to believers.

The apostles knew it was time for them to go out into the world and spread the Good News about Jesus. They would tell everyone that Jesus died for them, so their sins will be forgiven and they can live with him in heaven.

JOHN'S BEAUTIFUL DREAM
(John 19:26-27, Luke 1:28, Revelation 12)

When Jesus died on the cross, he asked his friend John to take care of his mother, Mary. Jesus also told his mother that John would be like a son to her.

Later, John saw a very special sign in heaven — a woman wearing the sun, with the moon under her feet. She had a crown of twelve stars. From this vision, John knew that Jesus had something special in mind for his mother.

On Mary's last day on earth, Jesus brought her, body and soul, into heaven. Here she reigns over all the saints as a queen. We celebrate the day that Mary was assumed into heaven on August 15, the Feast of the Assumption. Because her son, Jesus, is the King of Heaven, we call Mary our beautiful Queen of Heaven.

Mary has many other names, or titles. We call her Our Lady, Our Mother, Holy Queen, and many other beautiful phrases. She is the same Mary, no matter what title we call her.

Mary is the most special woman who ever lived. She was born without the stain of Adam and Eve's sin on her soul. Because she was born with no stain of sin, one of the names we call her is the Immaculate Conception. This means that her soul was always pure and clean, even from the time before she was born.

Just as Mary was the Mother of Jesus, we call her our mother, too. She knows her son wants all of us to come and live with him in heaven one day. She wants to help us know and love Jesus. She wants to bring us to the King. We pray to Mary and ask her to bring us close to Jesus.

THE PEOPLE OF JESUS

SIGNS AND WONDERS
(Acts 5)

When the Holy Spirit came on Pentecost, Jesus' friends, the apostles, knew that they must become brave missionaries. They

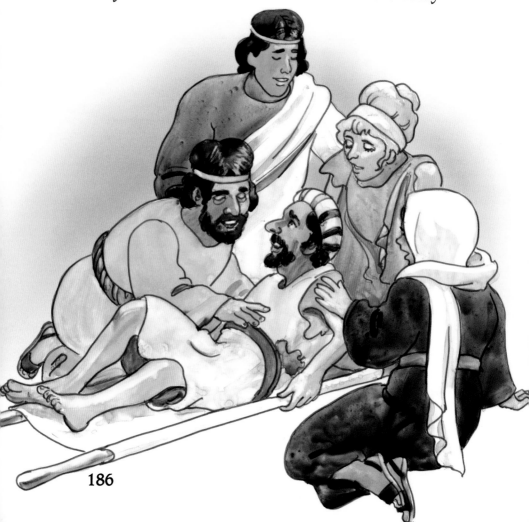

must go out into the world to tell the Good News: that Jesus died on the cross for us and rose from the dead.

As the apostles preached, many amazing

things happened. People who were sick became healthy again. All evil spirits were sent away.

At first, the apostles spread the Good News alone. But many new Christians wanted to be missionaries, too, helping share God's Word. We have a special name for those people who try to live the way Jesus taught us: We call them "disciples." Today, we are the disciples of Jesus when we share the Good News about God's love for us.

The apostles spread the Good News.

STEPHEN, THE FIRST MARTYR

(Acts 6-7)

Stephen was one of seven good, wise men the apostles chose to help do their work after Jesus ascended into heaven. Stephen began to preach and tell others about God's love. He healed the sick and served God's people.

Some men tried to argue with Stephen about his preaching, but they could not win against Stephen's holy wisdom. The men became jealous and spread lies about Stephen. They said he was breaking the law.

But Stephen told them that they were the ones who were breaking the law by the way they lived. This made the men furious, and they began to throw stones at Stephen. While the people threw stones at Stephen, he prayed and asked God to take his spirit to heaven. He also asked God to forgive the people for killing him.

Stephen was a faithful servant for God until he died, so God rewarded him by taking him to heaven. Stephen was our first martyr.

Stephen died for Christ.

MACEDONIA

Rome

ITALY

Paul

Thessalonica

Berea

Peter

ACHAIA

SICILY

Athens

Corinth

Cenchreae

Malta

CRET

PETER,
THE FIRST POPE
(Matthew 16:18-19)

N

Cyrene

192

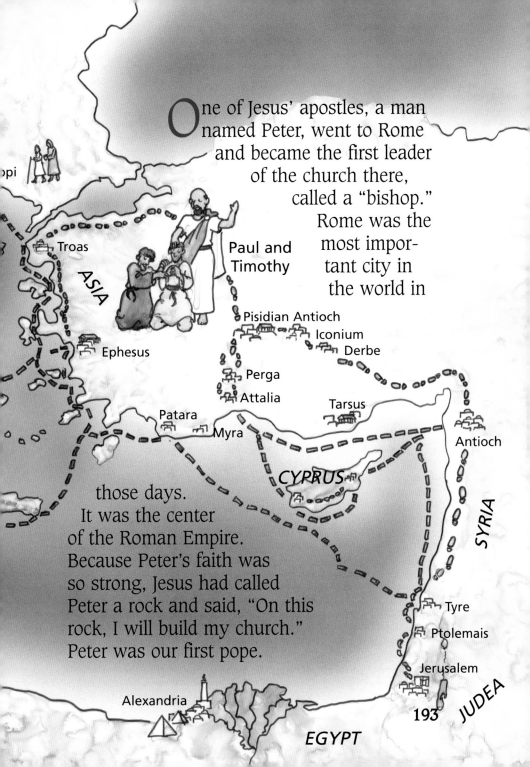

One of Jesus' apostles, a man named Peter, went to Rome and became the first leader of the church there, called a "bishop." Rome was the most important city in the world in those days. It was the center of the Roman Empire. Because Peter's faith was so strong, Jesus had called Peter a rock and said, "On this rock, I will build my church." Peter was our first pope.

Paul and Timothy

ASIA

Troas

Ephesus

Pisidian Antioch

Iconium

Derbe

Perga

Attalia

Tarsus

Patara

Myra

CYPRUS

Antioch

SYRIA

Tyre

Ptolemais

Jerusalem

JUDEA

Alexandria

193

EGYPT

SAUL BECOMES PAUL
(Acts 9:1-31)

Saul, a man from Tarsus, hated the new Christians. He began to round up the followers of Jesus and put them in prison. First,

he locked up the Christians in Jerusalem.
Next, Saul planned to go to a town named
Damascus to see if he could find more
Christians and take them back to jail in
Jerusalem.

As Saul was walking along the road to
Damascus, a big, bright light from heaven
suddenly flashed around him. The lightning

bolt knocked Saul to the ground. Then he heard a voice asking him, "Saul, why do you persecute me?"

Saul was frightened; he did not know where the voice was coming from. "Who are you?" he asked.

Again, the voice spoke. "I am Jesus, whom you are persecuting; but rise and enter the city, and you will be told what you are to do."

The men who were with Saul were stunned. They could hear the voice, too, but they couldn't see anyone. Then Saul realized that the bright light from heaven had made him blind. His friends led him into Damascus.

Then, Jesus appeared to a disciple in Damascus named Ananias and told him to visit Saul and cure his blindness. Ananias didn't want to go. He knew Saul had been putting Christians in prison. But the Lord told Ananias to obey, because God had chosen Saul to bring the Good News to many people.

So Ananias went to visit Saul and put his hands on him. Suddenly, Saul could see again! He was filled with the Holy Spirit and baptized as a Christian. Then he, too, became a disciple and began to preach and teach the Good News.

God chose Saul to tell the Good News.

PAUL TELLS EVERYONE
(Acts of the Apostles)

At first, all of Jesus' friends were members of the Jewish religion. Some of these apostles felt nervous about preaching to people who were not Jews, called "Gentiles." But Paul said that Jesus had died to save everyone, not just one group of people.

Paul began to travel from city to city. Whenever he found people who believed the Good News about Jesus, Paul started a church. Soon these believers began to call themselves "Christians," because they followed Christ. Paul wrote many long letters, called "epistles," to the Christians in the new churches, telling them how to live as Jesus wanted them to live.

Paul said Jesus died for everyone.

APOSTLES AND DISCIPLES
SPREAD THE GOOD NEWS
(Acts of the Apostles)

Other friends of Jesus went to the East, to important cities such as Alexandria and Antioch. Some of the apostles even went to cities outside the Roman Empire to begin churches in Persia and Germany.

The apostles and disciples wanted everyone to change from their old ways and convert to Christianity. The disciples were happy to tell other people about their friend, Jesus, and the way he taught them to love each other.

IV.
THE REST OF THE STORY

THE BIBLE AND
SACRED TRADITION

The Bible is a great and holy book. But it's
not the only way to learn about God's
wonderful love for us. Jesus told his friends,
called "apostles," to go tell everyone about

God's love. Some of the apostles wrote down this message in the Bible. But some of the apostles traveled and talked about God's plan. Their teachings are called Sacred, or Apostolic, Tradition.

We believe this Tradition is also the truth about God and his plan. The Tradition that Jesus taught the apostles does not change. Our Sacred Tradition and our Sacred Scripture teach us all that we need to know about God's love for us. They tell us how we should love God so that we can live with him forever.

The Bible and Sacred Tradition teach us how to live.

CHRISTIANS IN DANGER: THE EARLY CHURCH AND PERSECUTION
(Acts, Tradition)

For about 250 years, Christians lived in fear and danger. The Romans and other people worshiped false gods. But the Christians refused to worship these gods.

They wanted to worship only the one true God that Jesus taught us about.

Sometimes, the Romans ignored the Christians. Other times, the Romans punished them for not worshiping Roman gods. They beat the Christians, sold them as slaves, or even killed them by feeding them to hungry lions!

The Christians who were killed for being faithful to the one true God are called martyrs. They died for their beliefs. As a reward for being faithful, God took them straight to heaven. Sts. Cecelia, Agnes, Justin, and Lawrence were all brave young Christian martyrs. They were heroes, and even today we remember their names at Mass.

The martyrs died for their faith.

THE STORY CONTINUES

About 300 years after Jesus' death and Resurrection, a man named Constantine became the emperor of Rome. Constantine became a Christian, and said that all religions would be respected in the Roman Empire. The Christians in the Roman Empire would not be

beaten or punished. Christianity began to spread through the entire world.

Today, Christians still read the Bible to learn about God and his love for us all.

Christians read the Bible to learn about God and his love.

A Prayer to Prepare

Dear God,

Help me be still.
Show me how to sit quietly, God,
and pay attention to your important words.

Make me ready to be filled.
Open my ears, God, so your lessons can pour
in and find their way to my head and my
heart.

Help me do your will.
Give me some of your courage, God,
so I can share your stories with others and
show them what I've learned.

Amen.